Loveland,
Colorado

MW01041215

THIS MEANS LOVE

BIBLE STUDY
FOR WOMEN WHO WANT
TO MAKE A DIFFERENCE

Group resources really work!

This Group resource incorporates our R.E.A.L. approach to ministry. It reinforces a growing friendship with Jesus, encourages long-term learning, and results in life transformation, because it's:

Relational—Learner-to-learner interaction enhances learning and builds Christian friendships.

Experiential—What learners experience through discussion and action sticks with them up to 9 times longer than what they simply hear or read.

Applicable—The aim of Christian education is to equip learners to be both hearers and doers of God's Word.

Learner-based—Learners understand and retain more when the learning process takes into consideration how they learn best.

This Means Love Bible Study:
The Bible Study for Women Who Want to Make a Difference
Copyright © 2013 Group Publishing, Inc.

Visit our websites: group.com and group.com/women

This resource is brought to you by the wildly creative women's ministry team at Group.

Contributing authors: Amy Simpson, Amber Van Schooneveld, and Dee Ann Bragaw.

Unless otherwise indicated, all Scripture quotations are taken from the *Holy Bible*, New Living Translation, copyright © 1996, 2004, 2007 by Tyndale House Foundation. Used by permission of Tyndale House Publishers, Inc., Carol Stream, Illinois 60188. All rights reserved.

ISBN 978-1-4707-0242-7
Printed in the United States of America.
10 9 8 7 6 5 4 3 2 1   22 21 20 19 18 17 16 15 14 13

Contents

Introduction

*"Dear children, let's not merely say that we love
each other; let us show the truth by our actions."*
1 John 3:18

Together, we are embarking on a great adventure—the
adventure of serving God by serving others!

Most of us will agree that we want to serve God more. We
hear stories of women doing remarkable things for others
(from Mother Theresa, to that woman in our church) and
we think, "I want to make a difference, too. But I don't have
time. And I wouldn't know what to do even if I had the time!"
We heard your cry and created this simplified approach to
help you serve right where you are—in *your* church and in
your community.

Through the *This Means Love Bible Study,* we'll discover what
the Bible says about loving our neighbor as we study the
original love chapter, 1 Corinthians 13. Created to be used in
conjunction with the This Means Love Service Project Kit, this
Bible study will lead you deeper into Scripture and personal
reflection. Of course, this isn't just about reading and
discussion—it's about doing! This Means Love will encourage
you to take action on everything you study.

Each session starts with "Connecting With Each Other." These
lively discussions will help you grow in your faith and also
grow deeper friendships with the women in your group.

During the "Connecting With God" section, you'll dig deeper
into the Bible. At the same time, the Bible will dig deeper
into your heart. You'll gain a new perspective on serving and
realize that serving is more than showing up on Sunday.

The last section, "Connecting to Life," will encourage you to evaluate how you are going to put God's Word into action in your life. You'll be challenged to love and live in a bigger way, one that makes a positive impact on others.

How to use the *This Means Love Bible Study*

This Means Love Bible Study is the perfect companion to your This Means Love service project gatherings. We've left it up to you to choose the best way to use this book with your group. If you choose to meet just once a month, you may want to have your Bible study at the same time as your service project. Or if you prefer, you can meet every other week, alternating between your service project event and your Bible study. Each woman will need her own copy of this Bible study book.

To use this study with a group, select a leader for each session (or one person can lead throughout all six sessions). The leader will be responsible for gathering supplies needed for that session. The leader for the sessions can read aloud the text written in bold-face type. If you want to use this book independently, you can write out your answers to the "Connecting With Each Other" questions or meet with a friend and discuss the questions over coffee.

In each chapter, we've included a section called "Random Acts of Service." You can use these ideas in addition to the projects in the This Means Love Service Project Kit or let them inspire you to serve in other creative ways.

In addition, your group will need the This Means Love Service Project Kit. To facilitate the service project group, we recommend sharing the project guide folders and having a different woman host the gathering each month. Or if you prefer, one leader (or co-leaders) can lead each meeting. No group will be exactly the same—and that's OK! The important thing is to encourage women to participate in whatever capacity they feel comfortable.

At the back of this book (starting on page 57), you'll see the Service Project Notes section. Here is where you'll find the discussion questions, activities, and journaling space you'll use during the service project gatherings.

Let the adventure begin!

This Means Love lays the foundation for a fun and focused time of serving. Loving our neighbors doesn't have to be complicated—or time-consuming! In fact, it can be a way of life. Using the *This Means Love Bible Study* and Service Project Kit will be a springboard for you and your group to discover creative ways to show God's love. You'll be amazed at the huge rewards that come from simple acts of love. Let's get serving!

This Means Love

SESSION 1:
Nothing Without Love...

——————— Theme Verse ———————

"If I could speak all the languages of earth and of angels, but didn't love others, I would only be a noisy gong or a clanging cymbal. If I had the gift of prophecy, and if I understood all of God's secret plans and possessed all knowledge, and if I had such faith that I could move mountains, but didn't love others, I would be nothing. If I gave everything I have to the poor and even sacrificed my body, I could boast about it; but if I didn't love others, I would have gained nothing." (1 Corinthians 13:1-3)

Leader Prep
You'll be showing a scene from the movie *How the Grinch Stole Christmas*. Have a copy of the DVD ready, or search for it online. You'll want scenes 10 and 11 (47:12–55:25) on the DVD, starting with the scene titled "Holiday Cheermeister." The Mayor is just getting ready to present the cheermeister award. You can stop the scene right after the Grinch takes the stage with the mistletoe. You'll want to have it ready before your meeting.

Connecting With Each Other

It's your first week of gathering together to see what the Bible says about serving God and others. Take a few minutes to share your vision for this group and to hear from others why they've joined this conversation. Be sure everyone introduces themselves so you know each other's names. Then continue getting to know each other better with this discussion.

We all serve a variety of people in our everyday lives. And we have various motives for doing so. Introduce yourselves to each other, and discuss these questions:

- **Where are you already serving on a regular basis? All service counts! Consider how you serve your family, your boss and co-workers, organizations where you volunteer, your church, maybe even a pet you feed every day.**

- **What motivates you to serve in these ways?**

Connecting With God

Let's dig into those motives—the things that move us to action in service. Why, exactly, do we serve others?

Someone in your group can read 1 Corinthians 13:1-3 aloud:

If I could speak all the languages of earth and of angels, but didn't love others, I would only be a noisy gong or a clanging cymbal. If I had the gift of prophecy, and if I understood all of God's secret plans and possessed all knowledge, and if I had such faith that I could move mountains, but didn't love others, I would be nothing. If I gave everything I have to the poor and even sacrificed my body, I could boast about it; but if I didn't love others, I would have gained nothing.

This Scripture passage makes a strong point about the importance of doing what we do with love. It says that without love, even the best deeds are empty and meaningless.

Discuss these questions with your entire group. Jot your own thoughts in the spaces provided:

- **Can you think of any examples when doing impressive or sacrificial deeds might come across to others as "a noisy gong or a clanging cymbal"? Give examples.**

_____

_____

_____

- What are other motives people might have for acts of service?

_____

_____

_____

Let's consider an entertaining example of not-so-helpful service. In the movie *How the Grinch Stole Christmas* (the year-2000 version with Jim Carrey), little Cindy Lou Who tries to address her dissatisfaction with Christmas and mend the rift between the Whos and the Grinch by nominating the Grinch for the "Holiday Cheermeister" award. This award typically goes to the mayor of Whoville, but this year she convinces the townspeople to "honor" the Grinch with it because he is in need of holiday cheer. Watch to see how the town's efforts to honor the cheermeister affect the Grinch, who has been living in isolation for years after feeling rejected as a child.

Watch the "Holiday Cheermeister" scene from *How the Grinch Stole Christmas*, and then discuss the following questions:

- How did the Grinch seem to feel about this dubious honor?

- What sort of response do you think the people of Whoville were hoping for?

- Did anyone seem to benefit from this "act of service" toward the Grinch? Explain your opinion.

A different person from your group can read John 13:1-17 aloud:

> Before the Passover celebration, Jesus knew that his hour had come to leave this world and return to his Father. He had loved his disciples during his ministry on earth, and now he loved them to the very end. It was time for supper, and the devil had already prompted Judas, son of Simon Iscariot, to betray

Jesus. Jesus knew that the Father had given him authority over everything and that he had come from God and would return to God. So he got up from the table, took off his robe, wrapped a towel around his waist, and poured water into a basin. Then he began to wash the disciples' feet, drying them with the towel he had around him.

When Jesus came to Simon Peter, Peter said to him, "Lord, are you going to wash my feet?"

Jesus replied, "You don't understand now what I am doing, but someday you will."

"No," Peter protested, "you will never ever wash my feet!"

Jesus replied, "Unless I wash you, you won't belong to me."

Simon Peter exclaimed, "Then wash my hands and head as well, Lord, not just my feet!"

Jesus replied, "A person who has bathed all over does not need to wash, except for the feet, to be entirely clean. And you disciples are clean, but not all of you." For Jesus knew who would betray him. That is what he meant when he said, "Not all of you are clean."

After washing their feet, he put on his robe again and sat down and asked, "Do you understand what I was doing? You call me 'Teacher' and 'Lord,' and you are right, because that's what I am. And since I, your Lord and Teacher, have washed your feet, you ought to wash each other's feet. I have given you an example to follow. Do as I have done to you. I tell you the truth, slaves are not greater than their master. Nor is the messenger more important than the one who sends the message. Now that you know these things, God will bless you for doing them."

Let's consider these thoughts from the IVP New Testament Commentary on John:

"A Jewish text says this is something a Gentile slave could be required to do, but not a Jewish slave. On the other hand, footwashing is something wives did for their husbands, children for their parents, and disciples for their teachers. A level of intimacy is involved in these cases, unlike when Gentile slaves would do the washing. In Jesus' case, there is an obvious reversal of roles with his disciples. The one into whose hands the Father had given all now takes his disciples' feet into his hands to wash them." (Rodney A. Whitacre, IVP Academic, 2010)

- What do you think motivated Jesus to wash his disciples' feet?

- What might he have intended to communicate through this act of service?

- Jesus told his disciples to follow his example. Do you think he meant for us to follow that example too? If so, how?

Later that evening, after the foot washing, Jesus told his disciples, "So now I am giving you a new commandment: Love each other. Just as I have loved you, you should love each other. Your love for one another will prove to the world that you are my disciples" (John 13:34-35).

- What does Christian love look like when we act on it?

- Do our motives always change the type of response we get from the people we serve?

- Why would love motivate us to serve strangers? What kind of love is this?

Christian love shows itself in acts of service, just as Jesus set the example for us by washing his disciples' feet.

Connecting to Life

Spend a few minutes thinking about *your* noisy gongs and clanging symbols—ways you have served without love. Maybe you begrudgingly volunteer in your kids' school so people will think you're a good parent. Perhaps you have helped a friend or neighbor in the hope that he or she would do the same for you in the future. Or maybe you ask your friends how things are going just to provide an excuse to talk about yourself.

In the space provided below and on the next page, write some of these empty acts of service, and pray silently, confessing your unloving motives and asking God to fill you with his love for the acts of service he is calling you to.

As a group, close in prayer, asking God to call you to specific acts of service done in love and expecting nothing in return.

Thank your friends for joining this group, and be sure everyone knows when you'll be meeting next—whether it's for the next session of the Bible study or to participate in a service project together.

Random Acts of Service

Help the Homeless

Collect donations of bread or other food from local merchants. Offer to pick up and deliver the food on a regular basis to a shelter.

Remember the shelter when you have something to donate; most likely they can use it (or their residents can). For example, after a 50th anniversary party, one woman had three extra sheet cakes. She called the city mission, and they were happy to take the cakes to share with their clients.

This Means Love

SESSION 2:
Spreading the Love

Theme Verse

"Love is patient and kind." (1 Corinthians 13:4)

Leader Prep

You'll be showing a scene from the movie *Pay It Forward*. Have a copy of the DVD ready, or search for it online. You'll need scenes 9-10 starting with "Jerry's Leg Up" and part of scene 10, "That's the Idea." It starts with Helen Hunt finding Jim Caviezel in the garage and ends when the classroom scene is over. You'll want to have it cued up before your meeting.

Connecting With Each Other

Welcome everyone back to the group. If you have anyone new, be sure introductions are made and she feels welcomed. Then jump right in by showing the scenes from the movie *Pay It Forward*.

Discuss these questions with your entire group. Jot your thoughts in the spaces provided.

- **If you've seen this movie, describe what you remember about the results of young Trevor's idea.**

_____

_____

_____

- **Do you believe kindness really can change the world? Explain.**

_____

_____

_____

Connecting With God

First Corinthians 13:4 says, "Love is patient and kind." This verse provides a short but very important description of genuine love, the kind of love God has for us and that we are called to offer others. Have the group discuss the following:

- **What makes this verse deceptively simple?**

- **What are situations when you commonly run out of patience and kindness?**

Don't worry, you're not alone. We all find patience and kindness easier said than done. That's why we need God's Spirit to produce both of these virtues in us.

Read Galatians 5:22-23 aloud:

> _But the Holy Spirit produces this kind of fruit in our lives: love, joy, peace, patience, kindness, goodness, faithfulness, gentleness, and self-control. There is no law against these things!_

Discuss as a group, and allow time to write:

> _How do patience and kindness act as evidence of the Holy Spirit's influence in our lives?_

_____

_____

_____

This Means Love

- **What happens when we try to serve without patience and kindness?**

_____

_____

_____

- **How can we become walking examples of patience and kindness?**

_____

_____

_____

Have someone in the group read Luke 10:25-37 aloud:

> One day an expert in religious law stood up to test Jesus by asking him this question: "Teacher, what should I do to inherit eternal life?"
>
> Jesus replied, "What does the law of Moses say? How do you read it?"
>
> The man answered, "'You must love the Lord your God with all your heart, all your soul, all your strength, and all your mind.' And, 'Love your neighbor as yourself.'"
>
> "Right!" Jesus told him. "Do this and you will live!"
>
> The man wanted to justify his actions, so he asked Jesus, "And who is my neighbor?"
>
> Jesus replied with a story: "A Jewish man was traveling from Jerusalem down to Jericho, and he was attacked by bandits. They stripped him of his clothes, beat him up, and left him half dead beside the road.
>
> "By chance a priest came along. But when he saw the man lying there, he crossed to the other side of the road and passed him by. A Temple assistant walked

over and looked at him lying there, but he also passed by on the other side.

"Then a despised Samaritan came along, and when he saw the man, he felt compassion for him. Going over to him, the Samaritan soothed his wounds with olive oil and wine and bandaged them. Then he put the man on his own donkey and took him to an inn, where he took care of him. The next day he handed the innkeeper two silver coins, telling him, 'Take care of this man. If his bill runs higher than this, I'll pay you the next time I'm here.'

"Now which of these three would you say was a neighbor to the man who was attacked by bandits?" Jesus asked.

The man replied, "The one who showed him mercy."

Then Jesus said, "Yes, now go and do the same."

This story Jesus told, often called the Parable of the Good Samaritan, is a powerful demonstration of service.

- **From this account, what does it mean to show kindness and patience as we serve others?** Share thoughts as a group— but in the space provided, you can also write any thoughts you want to remember.

_____

_____

_____

- **Based on what we've discussed, would you say you're kind and patient when you serve? Why or why not? (And remember, it's OK to be honest in this group—no one is going to judge you!)**

_____

_____

_____

This Means Love

- **When has the Holy Spirit asked you to slow down and help someone, simply notice them, or show patience and kindness?**

_____

_____

_____

- **When has someone shown you unexpected patience and kindness?**

_____

_____

_____

- **What were the results of patience and kindness in these situations?**

_____

_____

_____

Just before this "love chapter" we're studying, the Apostle Paul wrote a metaphorical description of the body of Christ, including what it means to be interdependent with one another. Part of that chapter describes the way we're supposed to treat people who may often require patience and kindness from us.

Read 1 Corinthians 12:22-26 aloud:

In fact, some parts of the body that seem weakest and least important are actually the most necessary. And the parts we regard as less honorable are those we clothe with the greatest care. So we carefully protect those parts that should not be seen, while the more honorable parts do not require this special care.

So God has put the body together such that extra honor and care are given to those parts that have less dignity. This makes for harmony among the members, so that all the members care for each other. If one part suffers, all the parts suffer with it, and if one part is honored, all the parts are glad.

- **What might it look like to show special grace and honor to weaker members of our body?**

- **How do patience and kindness help us function as a group?**

- **How does a healthy body of Christ make a difference in the world?**

Serving others requires patience and kindness—we don't always see quick results or the kind of change we want to make in the world around us. We don't always like the people God calls us to serve. But in the Holy Spirit's power, we can serve others as Jesus asks us to.

Connecting to Life

Take a few minutes to think about what you have with you now. At the very least, you have the clothes you're wearing, perhaps some jewelry, and probably a purse or bag full of items. As you think about these belongings, consider how you might use them to serve others with kindness and patience. Write down at least three ways in the space provided.

_____

_____

_____

After everyone has had a few minutes to reflect, invite those who are willing to share just one of the things they wrote down.

Then, as a group, close in prayer, asking God to fill you with patience and kindness so you can effectively serve others in his power and in his name.

Random Acts of Service

Help for the Elderly

Adopt an elderly person (or couple), and check on them every week. Offer to pick up items from the store or pick up a prescription. This can be a huge help to an older couple.

Think of your elderly friends when baking cookies or making dinner. Prepare extra, and package it for them. It's a small action that can make a big difference! Offer to help wrap Christmas presents or to help write and mail birthday cards throughout the year.

This Means Love

SESSION 3:
Serving With Grace

─────── Theme Verse ───────

"Love is not jealous or boastful or proud or rude. It does not demand its own way. It is not irritable, and it keeps no record of being wronged." (1 Corinthians 13:4-5)

Leader Prep
If possible, have a paper shredder handy. If you don't have access to one, you'll need a few pairs of scissors for group members to share.

Connecting With Each Other

Welcome everyone to your time together. Begin with a time of discussion.

- **Do you work in a service industry? Have you had a service job in the past? For example, have you worked as a restaurant server, hotel employee, accountant, repair person, teacher, janitor, or financial advisor? If you have, tell the rest of the group about an experience that made you think your paycheck might not be worth enough to keep you in that job.**

- **If serving others is sometimes so unpleasant when we're getting paid, what makes us want to do it when we aren't getting paid?**

Connecting With God

Let's think about our *attitude* in serving others. Read
1 Corinthians 13:4-5 aloud:

> *Love is not jealous or boastful or proud or rude. It does not demand its own way. It is not irritable, and it keeps no record of being wronged.*

- **Tell about a time you "kept score" in a relationship? What happened?**

- **What makes us want to keep a "record of being wronged" or a record of what we've done right?**

When Christians serve, we should double-check to make sure we're serving with the right attitude. What is the Christian attitude toward service? It starts with the kind of love Paul described. Let's look in the Bible to find out more.

Read Matthew 20:25-28 aloud:

> *But Jesus called them together and said, "You know that the rulers in this world lord it over their people, and officials flaunt their authority over those under them. But among you it will be different. Whoever wants to be a leader among you must be your servant, and whoever wants to be first among you must become your slave. For even the Son of Man came not to be served but to serve others and to give his life as a ransom for many.*

- **How did Jesus change the idea of what it means to be a servant?**

- **When have you noticed leaders who serve the people under their authority? What happened? What did this mean to you personally?**

Read Luke 22:26-27 aloud:

> *But among you it will be different. Those who are the greatest among you should take the lowest rank, and the leader should be like a servant. Who is more important, the one who sits at the table or the one who serves? The one who sits at the table, of course. But not here! For I am among you as one who serves.*

This Means Love

- **How might the world be different if everyone followed these instructions about service?**

- **During his life on earth, how did Jesus demonstrate extraordinary service?**

Jesus is our ultimate example in service. And what he did went beyond what people could see or understand. He gave up unimaginable luxury and power in order to serve us, without the possibility that we could give him anything equivalent in return. Let's take a closer look at Jesus' attitude toward service.

Read Philippians 2:1-11 aloud:

> *Is there any encouragement from belonging to Christ? Any comfort from his love? Any fellowship together in the Spirit? Are your hearts tender and compassionate? Then make me truly happy by agreeing wholeheartedly with each other, loving one another, and working together with one mind and purpose.*
>
> *Don't be selfish; don't try to impress others. Be humble, thinking of others as better than yourselves. Don't look out only for your own interests, but take an interest in others, too.*
>
> *You must have the same attitude that Christ Jesus had.*
>
> *Though he was God, he did not think of equality with God as something to cling to.*
>
> *Instead, he gave up his divine privileges; he took the humble position of a slave and was born as a human being.*
>
> *When he appeared in human form, he humbled himself in obedience to God and died a criminal's death on a cross.*
>
> *Therefore, God elevated him to the place of highest honor and gave him the name above all other names, that at the name of Jesus every knee should bow, in heaven and on earth and under the earth, and every tongue confess that Jesus Christ is Lord, to the glory of God the Father.*

- What kind of rewards or payback do we often hope people will give us when we serve?

- What happens when people serve without expecting recognition or reward—without "keeping score"?

- What if you knew for sure that when you served, no one would ever say thank you, no one would help you in return, and you would receive no tax deduction? Would that change your motivation to serve?

Connecting to Life

Take a minute or two to consider what you're hoping to get in return for serving. List these rewards on page 29; then, as you're ready, follow the instructions on that page.

After everyone has completed this reflection, close your time in prayer, asking God to work in the hearts of each person here, bringing guidance and direction in this area of attitude.

Random Acts of Service

Love Your Neighborhood

Create an emergency contact list as a resource to share with neighbors. Include phone numbers for the local police or sheriff; domestic abuse, suicide, and rape hotlines; food pantry; and nearby churches (with contact names). Hand out to each neighbor and also post on local community bulletin boards.

Bring curb appeal by painting (or refreshing) street addresses on the curbs. This can be lifesaving in an emergency. All you need are stencils and spray paint. Check with each homeowner and get permission first, of course, and also check with the local municipality for any applicable laws. Before painting, be sure to dress for the occasion!

This Means Love

Rewards for Serving

Pray silently about your list, confessing your attitude to God and asking him to help you let go of the rewards you have been hoping for and to simply serve in his name.

When you're ready to let go, tear out this page and run it through the shredder or cut it up and throw away the pieces.

This Means Love

SESSION 4:
Righting the Wrongs

—— Theme Verse ——

"It does not rejoice about injustice but rejoices whenever the truth wins out." (1 Corinthians 13:6)

Leader Prep

Beforehand, you'll need to place a snack under or next to each person's seat. One person should receive an entire package of something tempting (like a whole bag of candy or a box of delicious cookies or crackers). The rest of the group should receive one small piece of something less appealing (like one plain cracker or a rice cake).

You'll also be showing a 6-minute documentary called "Grace's Story," produced by International Justice Mission. You'll want to have it ready before your meeting: youtube.com/intljusticemission

Connecting With Each Other

Each person should have a snack under or next to her seat; find yours now. Once you have your snack, go ahead and eat it. Be sure to notice what everyone else has.

As everyone is eating, discuss these questions:

- **If you were the person who received a bigger and better snack than everyone else, please explain why you chose to share or not to share with the rest of the group.**

- **Everyone else, what did you expect the person with the better snack to do with it? Why?**

- How did you all feel about the way the snacks were distributed?

The distribution of snacks in our group was unjust, as our world so often is. We have the power to pursue justice, but it's not always easy. Justice sometimes costs us something we would rather keep for ourselves.

Connecting With God

True love, like true service, seeks justice. First Corinthians 13:6 says, "It does not rejoice about injustice but rejoices whenever the truth wins out."

- How does our world sometimes rejoice in injustice?

The Bible has a lot to say about God's passion for justice. When we serve in his name, we must be committed to spreading justice, not rejoicing when people are mistreated, no matter how we feel about them. Let's look at one verse on this topic, Micah 6:8:

> O people, the Lord has told you what is good, and this is what he requires of you: to do what is right, to love mercy, and to walk humbly with your God.

- How would you say this verse is being demonstrated in your own life right now?

Let's keep this in mind as we watch a short documentary from International Justice Mission, describing situations going on in our world right now.

Watch "Grace's Story," and then discuss these questions:
- What's your immediate reaction after watching this story?

- What did Grace's justice cost her? What did it cost the people who took her case and won?

- When we hear stories of injustice in other countries, it might feel far away and that we can't really make a difference. How *can* our own small acts of service advance the cause of justice?

Acts 9:36-42 provides an example of a woman who worked for justice in her own small way. Let's read that:

There was a believer in Joppa named Tabitha (which in Greek is Dorcas). She was always doing kind things for others and helping the poor. About this time she became ill and died. Her body was washed for burial and laid in an upstairs room. But the believers had heard that Peter was nearby at Lydda, so they sent two men to beg him, "Please come as soon as possible!"

So Peter returned with them; and as soon as he arrived, they took him to the upstairs room. The room was filled with widows who were weeping and showing him the coats and other clothes Dorcas had made for them. But Peter asked them all to leave the room; then he knelt and prayed. Turning to the body he said, "Get up, Tabitha." And she opened her eyes! When she saw Peter, she sat up! He gave her his hand and helped her up. Then he called in the widows and all the believers, and he presented her to them alive.

The news spread through the whole town, and many believed in the Lord.

Usually when we read this passage we get pretty excited about the miracle of Tabitha coming back to life—which is downright miraculous! But let's talk about Tabitha for a moment.

- **From what others were saying about her, what kind of impact did Tabitha's service have? How was she seeking justice for others? What do you imagine this cost her?**

- **What might happen if all Christians today were to seek justice and share love so freely?**

Connecting to Life

As we consider the story of Grace and the story of Tabitha and the lives of others we know who are actively seeking justice for others, we see that often doing right has a cost— whether in our time, our finances, or in the burdens our hearts carry.

Let's take a little time to consider what pursuing justice might cost us. Let's make this a personal time of reflection. There are two questions on your page. Think on these, talk to God about his desires for you, and write your thoughts in the space provided.

- Think about what you might have to give up in order to pursue justice for someone else.

_____

_____

_____

_____

- Are you willing to pay that price to serve others in love?

_____

_____

_____

_____

Allow time for everyone to write.

As we close, pray on your own or with a partner. Ask God to give you the courage and love required to pay the price of justice for someone else.

Random Acts of Service

Freedom for Victims of Sex Trafficking

Host a fundraiser for an organization that works to free those caught in the sex trade. Groups have done everything from holding a rummage sale, to hosting a spaghetti dinner or barbeque, to having a silent auction with donated purses.

Some groups have handed out bars of soap to hotel managers. The bars of soap have a sex trafficking hotline phone number written on them. The soaps are then placed in rooms, in the hope that women in bondage will see the number and take a chance on a phone call that could deliver them. This should be done prayerfully and with the hotel's full participation.

This Means Love

SESSION 5:
Keeping the Faith

—————— Theme Verse ——————

"Love never gives up, never loses faith, is
always hopeful, and endures through every
circumstance." (1 Corinthians 13:7)

Leader Prep
You'll be reading a story about retired Nebraska
football coach Tom Osborne. For more background,
read this article: tinyurl.com/ThisMeansLove5

Connecting With Each Other

Welcome everyone, and hear any reports on service projects
you all have tried recently. What's gone well? What are
you excited about coming up? Then move ahead with this
week's content.

**Ready to really be honest here? Of course you are! Let's take
turns telling the rest of the group about a project, idea, or
resolution you just couldn't stick with, and why. For example,
maybe every January 1 for the last 15 years, you've resolved
to lose weight—and it's never happened! Or maybe you
have a craft project you've abandoned, a great plan you keep
thinking about but not acting on, or a degree you've never
finished. It's time to share!**

After everyone has had a turn to talk, continue.

**Achieving our goals requires commitment, endurance, and
hope. Sometimes we need those same qualities when we're
serving others in love.**

Connecting With God

First Corinthians 13:7 says, "Love never gives up, never loses faith, is always hopeful, and endures through every circumstance." This is a tall order, isn't it? We all know it's tough to stick with someone through the ups and downs of life. Fortunately, Jesus, who is our example of perfect love, always sticks with us.

Have someone in your group read Romans 8:35-38 aloud:

Can anything ever separate us from Christ's love? Does it mean he no longer loves us if we have trouble or calamity, or are persecuted, or hungry, or destitute, or in danger, or threatened with death? (As the Scriptures say, "For your sake we are killed every day; we are being slaughtered like sheep.") No, despite all these things, overwhelming victory is ours through Christ, who loved us.

And I am convinced that nothing can ever separate us from God's love. Neither death nor life, neither angels nor demons, neither our fears for today nor our worries about tomorrow—not even the powers of hell can separate us from God's love.

- **How does it feel to know that Christ's love will never let us go, walk away, or give up on us?**

- **How have you see Jesus demonstrate this kind of faithful love in your own life?**

In Jesus' life on earth, he demonstrated this kind of tenacious love in his relationship to Simon Peter, who was one of his closest friends and followers. Let's look at this story in three parts.

Have someone read Matthew 26:31-35 aloud:

Jesus told them, "Tonight all of you will desert me. For the Scriptures say,

'God will strike the Shepherd, and the sheep of the flock will be scattered.'

But after I have been raised from the dead, I will go ahead of you to Galilee and meet you there."

This Means Love

Peter declared, "Even if everyone else deserts you, I will never desert you."

Jesus replied, "I tell you the truth, Peter—this very night, before the rooster crows, you will deny three times that you even know me."

"No!" Peter insisted. "Even if I have to die with you, I will never deny you!" And all the other disciples vowed the same.

- **Why do you think Peter responded as he did to Jesus' claim that his disciples would desert him?**

- **Why do you think Jesus told his disciples they would desert him?**

Let's see what happened after Jesus was arrested and his disciples ran away.

Have someone else read Matthew 26:69-75 aloud:

Meanwhile, Peter was sitting outside in the courtyard. A servant girl came over and said to him, "You were one of those with Jesus the Galilean."

But Peter denied it in front of everyone. "I don't know what you're talking about," he said.

Later, out by the gate, another servant girl noticed him and said to those standing around, "This man was with Jesus of Nazareth."

Again Peter denied it, this time with an oath. "I don't even know the man," he said.

A little later some of the other bystanders came over to Peter and said, "You must be one of them; we can tell by your Galilean accent."

Peter swore, "A curse on me if I'm lying—I don't know the man!" And immediately the rooster crowed.

Suddenly, Jesus' words flashed through Peter's mind: "Before the rooster crows, you will deny three times that you even know me." And he went away, weeping bitterly.

- As you read of Peter and consider this moment when he hears the rooster and begins to weep, how do you relate to him?

Later, after Jesus' death and resurrection, he appeared to the disciples and had some special words for Peter.

Have another person read John 21:15-17 aloud:

> *After breakfast Jesus asked Simon Peter, "Simon son of John, do you love me more than these?"*
>
> *"Yes, Lord," Peter replied, "you know I love you."*
>
> *"Then feed my lambs," Jesus told him.*
>
> *Jesus repeated the question: "Simon son of John, do you love me?"*
>
> *"Yes, Lord," Peter said, "you know I love you."*
>
> *"Then take care of my sheep," Jesus said.*
>
> *A third time he asked him, "Simon son of John, do you love me?"*
>
> *Peter was hurt that Jesus asked the question a third time. He said, "Lord, you know everything. You know that I love you."*
>
> *Jesus said, "Then feed my sheep."*

- **What do you think Jesus meant by "feed my sheep"?**

- **What did this conversation give Peter?**

- **How did Peter's life later show evidence that he was changed by this conversation?**

Jesus didn't give up on Peter before or after his public betrayal — and he doesn't give up on us. This kind of faithfulness is life-changing and can give us hope and a purpose. God wants us to extend this same gift to other people.

Have someone in the group volunteer to read the following illustration of what can happen when we refuse to give up on others.

The Power of Redemption

You've probably heard of Tom Osborne, former Nebraska football coach and college football legend. You may not have heard of Ricky Simmons.

Ricky Simmons played for Coach Osborne from 1979 to 1983. He went on to play pro football, including one year with the Atlanta Falcons; but his addiction to cocaine brought his career to a screeching halt. His third and final prison sentence landed him in Tecumseh, Nebraska, just one hour from Memorial Stadium where he spent his glory days as a Nebraska Cornhusker. His addiction had destroyed his life and his career. To make the situation even harder to bear, the prison guards taunted him for his fall from football hero to drug addict.

In 2008, the guard approached Ricky's cell carrying a letter with the red Nebraska "N" insignia. It was from Coach Osborne. It contained a letter that would change the course of Ricky's life, although in his present state he was almost too ashamed to even open it. He had disappointed everyone in his life, including his former coach. Finally, he mustered up enough courage to open the letter and read two short lines:

"Dear Ricky, I know your parents believed in you, and I believe in you. Upon your release if there's anything I can do to help you, feel free to contact me. Tom Osborne."

Simmons read the letter over and over, finally falling to his knees in total surrender. He gave his life to Christ in that moment: "When I finally stood up, I knew I was still in prison, but the gates had swung wide open in my mind. T.O. still believed in me." Tom's words of encouragement had been the catalyst he needed to let go of the past and get his life going in the right direction again.

Simmons remained in prison for the next 18 months, but his outlook was completely changed. Before this, his addiction had him on the path of destruction with no way out. No life. No job. No future. Now he began to hope again. He knew with Coach Osborne's help he could create a different future for himself and for his son.

It wasn't an easy road, but with Coach Osborne on his side, Ricky pursued his license in drug and alcohol counseling and his dream of becoming a motivational speaker. Today, Ricky is an addiction counselor and speaks at high schools, churches, and youth organizations. He stays in touch with Tom on a weekly basis; according to Ricky: "I owe my second life to him."

Discuss the following questions:

- **What do you think inspired Coach Osborne to write the letter? Why might he have believed in Ricky Simmons?**

- **When has someone believed in you beyond what you thought possible?**

- **How could we give this same gift to the people we serve?**

If we believe in God's power and redemption and we recognize how he has given it to us, we'll know that *no one* is beyond the reach of his grace and mercy. We'll continue to love in his name, even when we're tempted to give up on people.

Connecting to Life

Let's spend a few moments in silence, thinking of people who need God's redemption and who you're tempted to give up on. Acknowledge that you need God's help to believe he can redeem these people.

Allow time for quiet reflection. Write any notes you want to remember here.

_____

_____

_____

_____

_____

_____

_____

_____

_____

_____

After a few minutes, close by praying as a group, without mentioning names, asking God for faith to keep loving and serving in his name when you're ready to give up.

Random Acts of Service

Help for Hurting Families

Prepare meals for the parents of seriously ill children. Contact your children's hospital, and ask what opportunities there are to serve in this way. Perhaps you can provide a meal to those staying in a hotel or send a gift card to a local restaurant. The Ronald McDonald home accepts volunteers to come in to cook and serve meals.

SESSION 6:
Making a Difference

--------- Theme Verse ---------

"Prophecy and speaking in unknown languages and special knowledge will become useless. But love will last forever! Now our knowledge is partial and incomplete, and even the gift of prophecy reveals only part of the whole picture! But when the time of perfection comes, these partial things will become useless. When I was a child, I spoke and thought and reasoned as a child. But when I grew up, I put away childish things. Now we see things imperfectly, like puzzling reflections in a mirror, but then we will see everything with perfect clarity. All that I know now is partial and incomplete, but then I will know everything completely, just as God now knows me completely. Three things will last forever—faith, hope, and love—and the greatest of these is love." (1 Corinthians 13:8-13)

Leader Prep
You'll need to be able to play the song "Revelation Song" performed by Kari Jobe or Jesus Culture, which can be found on CD, iTunes, Spotify, or YouTube.

Connecting With Each Other

Welcome everyone warmly, and then get started.

Think about the way you saw the world when you were a child. Tell the group about some misunderstandings you had. For example, maybe you thought Disney World was another

planet. Perhaps you misunderstood the lyrics to a song. Or maybe you thought Sesame Street was an actual street in your town. How did you learn the truth?

Allow time for each person to share, and then continue. **The Bible tells us that someday we will know and understand the truth in ways we can't now—our eyes and our minds will be opened to a greater understanding of reality.**

Connecting With God

Invite someone in your group to read 1 Corinthians 13:8-13 aloud:

Prophecy and speaking in unknown languages and special knowledge will become useless. But love will last forever! Now our knowledge is partial and incomplete, and even the gift of prophecy reveals only part of the whole picture! But when the time of perfection comes, these partial things will become useless.

When I was a child, I spoke and thought and reasoned as a child. But when I grew up, I put away childish things. Now we see things imperfectly, like puzzling reflections in a mirror, but then we will see everything with perfect clarity. All that I know now is partial and incomplete, but then I will know everything completely, just as God now knows me completely.

Three things will last forever—faith, hope, and love— and the greatest of these is love.

- **In what ways do you think our knowledge is "partial and incomplete"?**

- **How should the truth that "love will last forever" change the way we live?**

Even though we can't see the full picture now, it's all around us— and our lives are part of it. We are all part of God's great plan.

In his classic book *Mere Christianity*, C. S. Lewis wrote, "Christianity is the story of how the rightful king has landed, you might say landed in disguise, and is calling us all to take part in a great campaign of sabotage."

This Means Love

- How does this description compare to your own understanding of Christianity?

- What would you say is your part in this "great campaign of sabotage"?

Let's look at some examples of people who did their part to follow God when faced with a choice, even though they couldn't see the bigger picture of God's plan.

For this part of the study, form four groups (a group can be one person). Each group should read one of the following Bible passages and then consider the questions and prepare to share with the rest of the group what they learn.

Group 1: The Boy Who Brought Lunch
Read John 6:1-13:

Jesus crossed over to the far side of the Sea of Galilee, also known as the Sea of Tiberias. A huge crowd kept following him wherever he went, because they saw his miraculous signs as he healed the sick. Then Jesus climbed a hill and sat down with his disciples around him. (It was nearly time for the Jewish Passover celebration.) Jesus soon saw a huge crowd of people coming to look for him. Turning to Philip, he asked, "Where can we buy bread to feed all these people?" He was testing Philip, for he already knew what he was going to do.

Philip replied, "Even if we worked for months, we wouldn't have enough money to feed them!"

Then Andrew, Simon Peter's brother, spoke up. "There's a young boy here with five barley loaves and two fish. But what good is that with this huge crowd?"

"Tell everyone to sit down," Jesus said. So they all sat down on the grassy slopes. (The men alone numbered about 5,000.) Then Jesus took the loaves, gave thanks to God, and distributed them to the people. Afterward he did the same with the fish. And they all ate as much

as they wanted. After everyone was full, Jesus told his disciples, "Now gather the leftovers, so that nothing is wasted." So they picked up the pieces and filled twelve baskets with scraps left by the people who had eaten from the five barley loaves."

- **Why do you think the boy gave his lunch willingly? Can you think of a time someone gave so willingly to you?**

_____

_____

_____

_____

- **What were the long-term and ongoing results of this boy's choice?**

_____

_____

_____

_____

- **How does this story show that the boy's faithfulness was part of God's plan?**

_____

_____

_____

_____

This Means Love

Group 2: The Widow at Zarephath

Read 1 Kings 17:8-24:

> Then the Lord said to Elijah, "Go and live in the village of Zarephath, near the city of Sidon. I have instructed a widow there to feed you."
>
> So he went to Zarephath. As he arrived at the gates of the village, he saw a widow gathering sticks, and he asked her, "Would you please bring me a little water in a cup?" As she was going to get it, he called to her, "Bring me a bite of bread, too."
>
> But she said, "I swear by the Lord your God that I don't have a single piece of bread in the house. And I have only a handful of flour left in the jar and a little cooking oil in the bottom of the jug. I was just gathering a few sticks to cook this last meal, and then my son and I will die."
>
> But Elijah said to her, "Don't be afraid! Go ahead and do just what you've said, but make a little bread for me first. Then use what's left to prepare a meal for yourself and your son. For this is what the Lord, the God of Israel, says: There will always be flour and olive oil left in your containers until the time when the Lord sends rain and the crops grow again!"
>
> So she did as Elijah said, and she and Elijah and her family continued to eat for many days. There was always enough flour and olive oil left in the containers, just as the Lord had promised through Elijah.
>
> Some time later the woman's son became sick. He grew worse and worse, and finally he died. Then she said to Elijah, "O man of God, what have you done to me? Have you come here to point out my sins and kill my son?"
>
> But Elijah replied, "Give me your son." And he took the child's body from her arms, carried him up the stairs to the room where he was staying, and laid the body on his bed. Then Elijah cried out to the Lord, "O Lord my God, why have you brought tragedy to this widow who has opened her home to me, causing her son to die?"

And he stretched himself out over the child three times and cried out to the Lord, "O Lord my God, please let this child's life return to him." The Lord heard Elijah's prayer, and the life of the child returned, and he revived! Then Elijah brought him down from the upper room and gave him to his mother. "Look!" he said. "Your son is alive!"

Then the woman told Elijah, "Now I know for sure that you are a man of God, and that the Lord truly speaks through you."

- **What could have motivated this woman to give, even in her dire situation? When have you seen someone give so sacrificially?**

\
\
\
\

- **How did the widow see blessings from her service to Elijah?**

\
\
\
\

- **What were the long-term and ongoing results of her choice?**

\
\
\
\

This Means Love

- **How does this story show that the widow's act of faith was part of God's plan?**

_____

_____

_____

_____

Group 3: Rahab

Read Joshua 2:1-16:

> Then Joshua secretly sent out two spies from the
> Israelite camp at Acacia Grove. He instructed them,
> "Scout out the land on the other side of the Jordan
> River, especially around Jericho." So the two men
> set out and came to the house of a prostitute named
> Rahab and stayed there that night.
>
> But someone told the king of Jericho, "Some Israelites
> have come here tonight to spy out the land." So the
> king of Jericho sent orders to Rahab: "Bring out the
> men who have come into your house, for they have
> come here to spy out the whole land."
>
> Rahab had hidden the two men, but she replied, "Yes,
> the men were here earlier, but I didn't know where
> they were from. They left the town at dusk, as the
> gates were about to close. I don't know where they
> went. If you hurry, you can probably catch up with
> them." (Actually, she had taken them up to the roof and
> hidden them beneath bundles of flax she had laid out.)
> So the king's men went looking for the spies along the
> road leading to the shallow crossings of the Jordan
> River. And as soon as the king's men had left, the gate
> of Jericho was shut.
>
> Before the spies went to sleep that night, Rahab went
> up on the roof to talk with them. "I know the Lord
> has given you this land," she told them. "We are all

afraid of you. Everyone in the land is living in terror. For we have heard how the Lord made a dry path for you through the Red Sea when you left Egypt. And we know what you did to Sihon and Og, the two Amorite kings east of the Jordan River, whose people you completely destroyed. No wonder our hearts have melted in fear! No one has the courage to fight after hearing such things. For the Lord your God is the supreme God of the heavens above and the earth below.

"Now swear to me by the Lord that you will be kind to me and my family since I have helped you. Give me some guarantee that when Jericho is conquered, you will let me live, along with my father and mother, my brothers and sisters, and all their families."

"We offer our own lives as a guarantee for your safety," the men agreed. "If you don't betray us, we will keep our promise and be kind to you when the Lord gives us the land."

Then, since Rahab's house was built into the town wall, she let them down by a rope through the window. "Escape to the hill country," she told them. "Hide there for three days from the men searching for you. Then, when they have returned, you can go on your way."

- **Based on what you've read of Rahab, where do you think the faith she displayed came from?**

_____

_____

_____

_____

- How did her tremendous risk end up blessing her?

_____

_____

_____

_____

- What were the long-term and ongoing results of her choice?

_____

_____

_____

_____

- How does this story show that Rahab's act of faith was part of God's plan?

_____

_____

_____

_____

Group 4: Ruth

Read Ruth 3:1-13:

> One day Naomi said to Ruth, "My daughter, it's time
> that I found a permanent home for you, so that you will
> be provided for. Boaz is a close relative of ours, and
> he's been very kind by letting you gather grain with his
> young women. Tonight he will be winnowing barley at
> the threshing floor. Now do as I tell you—take a bath
> and put on perfume and dress in your nicest clothes.
> Then go to the threshing floor, but don't let Boaz see

you until he has finished eating and drinking. Be sure to notice where he lies down; then go and uncover his feet and lie down there. He will tell you what to do."

"I will do everything you say," Ruth replied. So she went down to the threshing floor that night and followed the instructions of her mother-in-law.

After Boaz had finished eating and drinking and was in good spirits, he lay down at the far end of the pile of grain and went to sleep. Then Ruth came quietly, uncovered his feet, and lay down. Around midnight Boaz suddenly woke up and turned over. He was surprised to find a woman lying at his feet! "Who are you?" he asked.

"I am your servant Ruth," she replied. "Spread the corner of your covering over me, for you are my family redeemer."

"The Lord bless you, my daughter!" Boaz exclaimed. "You are showing even more family loyalty now than you did before, for you have not gone after a younger man, whether rich or poor. Now don't worry about a thing, my daughter. I will do what is necessary, for everyone in town knows you are a virtuous woman. But while it's true that I am one of your family redeemers, there is another man who is more closely related to you than I am. Stay here tonight, and in the morning I will talk to him. If he is willing to redeem you, very well. Let him marry you. But if he is not willing, then as surely as the Lord lives, I will redeem you myself! Now lie down here until morning."

- **Naomi's instructions seem so odd to us, yet Ruth obeyed. When have you obeyed in an unusual way—or when have you seen someone else do so?**

_____

_____

_____

This Means Love

- **How did Ruth's bold actions bless others? What were the long-term and ongoing results of her choice?**

_____

_____

_____

_____

- **How does this story show that Ruth's self-sacrifice was part of God's plan?**

_____

_____

_____

_____

After each group has read and discussed their sections, take turns sharing with the other groups what you learned from your Bible passage and your discussion questions.

Isaiah 55:8-9 tells us, " 'My thoughts are nothing like your thoughts,' says the Lord. 'And my ways are far beyond anything you could imagine. For just as the heavens are higher than the earth, so my ways are higher than your ways and my thoughts higher than your thoughts.' "

Because of God's plan, the boy's shared lunch became a powerful demonstration of Jesus' divinity. The widow at Zarephath not only received her son back from the dead but enabled the powerful prophetic ministry of Elijah. Rahab, Matthew 1:5 tells us, became the mother of Boaz. After Ruth and Boaz married, Ruth became the mother of Jesse, father of King David. Both women are honored as ancestors of Jesus himself.

God has plans far beyond what we can see. We are all part of God's big plan, all on a mission from him. It's not our job to change the world, but to be faithful to what he asks of us. He is more than capable of taking care of the rest.

Connecting to Life

To finish this study, play "Revelation Song" from YouTube. Together, worship aloud or silently.

Then close by reading this prayer aloud together:

Lord, we acknowledge that it's your job to save the world and that you have a magnificent plan.

We look forward to the day when your plan will be revealed.

We commit to be faithful in what you call us to do. God, we trust you with your plan. Amen.

Random Acts of Service

Helping Single Parents

Offer free babysitting once a month, either in someone's home or the church nursery. This can be a great help to a busy mom who may have errands to run or just needs a break!

Sponsor a church-wide campaign to collect gift cards for single parents in need. Often people have cards sitting around that they haven't used. Set up a basket at the information desk for donations. Mail these out to those who need assistance.

This Means Love

Service Project Notes:
Home-Less. Not Loved-Less

"Those who shut their ears to the cries of the poor will be ignored in their own time of need." (Proverbs 21:13)

"Blessed are those who are generous, because they feed the poor." (Proverbs 22:9)

"The godly care about the rights of the poor; the wicked don't care at all." (Proverbs 29:7)

"She extends a helping hand to the poor and opens her arms to the needy." (Proverbs 31:20)

Here's what happened when I gave a gift to someone in need:

_____

_____

_____

_____

_____

_____

_____

_____

_____

_____

_____

_____

_____

Stuffed and Fluffed With Love

"But Jesus spoke to them at once. 'Don't be afraid,' he said. 'Take courage! I am here!'" (Mark 6:50)

"What shall we say about such wonderful things as these? If God is for us, who can ever be against us? Since he did not spare even his own Son but gave him up for us all, won't he also give us everything else?" (Romans 8:31-32)

"I am leaving you with a gift—peace of mind and heart. And the peace I give is a gift the world cannot give. So don't be troubled or afraid." (John 14:27)

"This is my command—be strong and courageous! Do not be afraid or discouraged. For the Lord your God is with you wherever you go." (Joshua 1:9)

Loveable Lunches

In 1 Corinthians 12:7 it says, "A spiritual gift is given to each of us so we can help each other."

- **Write one of your "gifts" here. It can be a talent, skill, or just an interest.**

_____

- **How can you use this gift to serve others?**

_____

_____

_____

_____

_____

_____

_____

_____

_____

_____

_____

_____

_____

_____

White gLove Treatment

"Your love has given me much joy and comfort, my brother, for your kindness has often refreshed the hearts of God's people." (Philemon 1:7)

- **Here's everything I did this week:**

_____

_____

_____

_____

_____

_____

_____

- **Something that would make me feel refreshed is:**

_____

_____

_____

_____

_____

_____

_____

I commit to making time to refresh myself this month.

_____   _____
Date   Signature

This Means Love

Prayers of Love

Here are ways you can take further action in the fight against sex trafficking.

Get equipped with knowledge. Learn more about this issue at love146.org/slavery.

Take a pledge to help end slavery. Sign your name at enditmovement.com/.

Get involved in your own state. If you want to find out how you can get involved in combating sex trafficking in your state, go to polarisproject.org/state-map.

Raise funds to stop traffickers. You could hold your own 5K or even ask for donations instead of gifts for your birthday. To learn more about raising funds for International Justice Mission, a human rights agency that helps rescue victims, go to ijmfreedommaker.org/.

My thoughts and prayers:

_____

_____

_____

_____

_____

_____

_____

_____

_____

_____

_____

_____

Love Is Cool!

"For I will pour out water to quench your thirst." (Isaiah 44:3)

- **In what ways are people in our neighborhoods thirsty for God's presence?**

_____

_____

_____

_____

_____

- **How can we be like a cool drink of water or glass of refreshing lemonade to our neighbors?**

_____

_____

_____

_____

_____

- **What's one thing you can do this week to refresh your neighbors?**

_____

_____

_____

_____

_____

Love to Get Your Hands Dirty

"Use your hands for good hard work, and then give generously to others in need." (Ephesians 4:28)

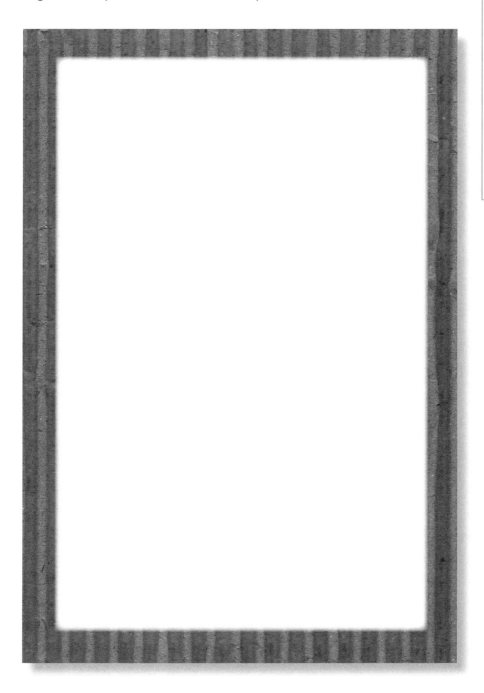

You Look Lovely

According to SingleMotherGuide.com, in 2011 unemployment was 15% for unmarried, divorced, or separated moms. That's about **1.2 million single mothers** who wanted a job but couldn't find one and who had children under 18 years old.

I'm sure most of us know a single mom who is in a tough financial situation. The Bible tells us to care for widows and orphans. While many single moms aren't technically "widows," Jesus wants us to care for them just the same.

Write the name or names of those you know who are looking for employment. Pray for them throughout the month.

_____

_____

_____

_____

_____

_____

_____

_____

_____

_____

_____

_____

_____

_____

_____

This Means Love

Love and Lysol

Many times in the Bible, followers of Jesus call him "Teacher." (You can check out Matthew 22:36, Mark 10:17-20, and Luke 9:38 for a few examples.) If Jesus was a teacher in your local school, how would you want to honor him?

Read Matthew 25:34-40 together:

> "Then the King will say to those on his right, 'Come, you who are blessed by my Father, inherit the Kingdom prepared for you from the creation of the world. For I was hungry, and you fed me. I was thirsty, and you gave me a drink. I was a stranger, and you invited me into your home. I was naked, and you gave me clothing. I was sick, and you cared for me. I was in prison, and you visited me.'

> "Then these righteous ones will reply, 'Lord, when did we ever see you hungry and feed you? Or thirsty and give you something to drink? Or a stranger and show you hospitality? Or naked and give you clothing? When did we ever see you sick or in prison and visit you?'

> "And the King will say, 'I tell you the truth, when you did it to one of the least of these my brothers and sisters, you were doing it to me!' "

- **How does this verse give you perspective on serving teachers and children—and what this means to Jesus?**

_____

_____

_____

_____

_____

_____

_____

Love-o'-Lantern

- **What types of serving are you most comfortable with?**

_____

_____

_____

_____

_____

_____

_____

_____

_____

- **What types of things scare you the most?**

_____

_____

_____

_____

_____

_____

_____

_____

_____

This Means Love

BeLoved Books

"You are the light of the world—like a city on a hilltop that cannot be hidden. No one lights a lamp and then puts it under a basket. Instead, a lamp is placed on a stand, where it gives light to everyone in the house. In the same way, let your good deeds shine out for all to see, so that everyone will praise your heavenly Father." (Matthew 5:14-16)

- **In what ways could our simple act of giving a book be a light to children in need and to their families?**

_____

_____

_____

_____

_____

_____

_____

_____

_____

_____

_____

_____

_____

_____

_____

Wrapped in Love

"And the result of God's gracious gift is very different from the result of that one man's sin. For Adam's sin led to condemnation, but God's free gift leads to our being made right with God, even though we are guilty of many sins." (Romans 5:16)

"For the wages of sin is death, but the free gift of God is eternal life through Christ Jesus our Lord." (Romans 6:23)

- **How has God's free gift changed your life?**

_____

_____

_____

_____

_____

_____

- **How has this free gift motivated you to give freely to others through your actions of service?**

_____

_____

_____

_____

_____

_____

_____

Additional Notes:

Additional Notes:

This Means Love

Additional Notes:

Additional Notes: